Just a Season

KEMI FALOYE

WESTBOW°
PRESS
A DIVISION OF THOMAS NELSON
& ZONDERVAN

Scripture quotations taken from the Holy Bible, New Living Translation, copyright 1996, 2004. Used by permission of Tyndale House Publishers, Inc., Wheaton, Illinois 60189. All rights reserved.

Scriptures taken from the Holy Bible, New International Version®, NIV®. Copyright © 1973, 1978, 1984, 2011 by Biblica, Inc.™ Used by permission of Zondervan. All rights reserved worldwide. www.zondervan.com The "NIV" and "New International Version" are trademarks registered in the United States Patent and Trademark Office by Biblica, Inc.™ All rights reserved.

Scripture taken from the New King James Version. Copyright 1979, 1980, 1982 by Thomas Nelson, inc. Used by permission. All rights reserved.

Scripture quotations are from The Holy Bible, English Standard Version® (ESV®), copyright © 2001 by Crossway, a publishing ministry of Good News Publishers. Used by permission. All rights reserved.

Scripture quotations taken from the New American Standard Bible*, Copyright © 1960, 1962, 1963, 1968, 1971, 1972, 1973, 1975, 1977, 1995 by The Lockman Foundation. Used by permission." (www.Lockman.org)

Scripture taken from the *Amplified Bible*, Copyright © 1954, 1958, 1962, 1964, 1965, 1987 by The Lockman Foundation. Used by permission.

All Scripture quotations in this publications are from **The Message**. Copyright (c) by Eugene H. Peterson 1993, 1994, 1995, 1996, 2000, 2001, 2002. Used by permission of NavPress Publishing Group.

WestBow Press books may be ordered through booksellers or by contacting:
WestBow Press
A Division of Thomas Nelson & Zondervan
1663 Liberty Drive
Bloomington, IN 47403
www.westbowpress.com
1 (866) 928-1240

ISBN: 978-1-4908-4709-2 (sc)
ISBN: 978-1-4908-4711-5 (hc)
ISBN: 978-1-4908-4710-8 (e)
Library of Congress Control Number: 2014914000

Printed in the United States of America.

WestBow Press rev. date: 08/20/2014

Contents

Dedication

This book is dedicated to my son,
Theodore Daniel Tomiwa Faloye,
Indeed your testimony of God's faithfulness would
Remain an inspiration to many.

Life isn't about waiting for the storm to pass,
it's about learning to dance in the rain.

Vivian Greene

Reviews

I looked forward to Kemi's book getting published with a great sense of anticipation, because I know her story.

When I met Kemi, she was a gangly single girl and I have had the pleasure of seeing her transition from the youthful optimism of a newly married young lady into a maturing mother. Most importantly, because of her journey through 11 miscarriages, I have seen her become a woman of God. In this book, she is open about the pain, isolation and suffering that is part of that journey. She discusses its impact on her relationship with God and other people in her life, and how we can interact appropriately with those who are experiencing delay in childbirth. Her story also makes clear the importance of medical intervention working hand in hand with a life of faith to achieve the impossible.

It's been a lesson just to watch her life and see her journey through repeated loss and pain into a place of fulfilled promise and victory.

Her story is instructive because she wasn't broken. Although sometimes out for the count, she wasn't down for long. Her resilience and faith is laudable, and she is an inspiration to many because of it.

Far from being a book about delay in childbirth, this is a book about faith in God in impossible circumstances. In this book you will gain invaluable knowledge to secure the fulfilment of the promises of God in every area of your life.

Pastor Bimbo Fola-Alade
Family Life Pastor
Trinity Chapel, London.

The Kemi I initially met at church and Kemi the mother are definitively two different people. Such muscles! Physically they both look the same, but the latter person is a trained and qualified warrior with battle scars to show for it!

As I read the book, I kept seeing a picture in my mind, of a young frail teenager pushing against a seemingly immovable wall for so many years and then being frustrated at the lack of motion in the wall, gets a glimpse of himself in the mirror only to see a fully developed wrestler staring back at him. Kemi has grown in wisdom, definitely in stature, evidently in favour with God and through this book, favour with men.

Kemi, thank you for this book, it helps us understand our season of preparation for the good things God has in store for us.

Mr Akin Salami
CEO, OHTV

Having been personally involved from the onset of Kemi's trial (ordeal) it gives me utmost pleasure to celebrate the fact that she has overcome it but more so as she leads others who are facing a similar predicament to their ultimate victory with her testimony as a focal point.

I have taught for years that you have to go through a mess to have a truly authentic message & each chapter in the book builds a picture of how to supernaturally overcome a situation that has continually perplexed medical science.

I wholeheartedly recommend this book to anyone who is facing a trial that has bought them to the point where human endeavour has failed them & offers no further solution as you will learn how supernatural nuggets via the word of God & the dedication of His servants can release people into fulfilled destiny through faith.

Enjoy the read!
Dr. Sola Fola-Alade
Senior Pastor, Trinity Chapel, London

Kemi Faloye's book "Just a Season" held me spellbound for the 90 straight minutes it took me to devour it from cover to cover. What an inspiring and amazing testimony of God's faithfulness! What an awesome reassurance that in spite of all we may go through during our journey to motherhood, our Heavenly Father is right there by our side, holding our hand, encouraging us to have faith, confess the word, believe and then leave the rest to Him.

11 miscarriages in almost 6 years! Yet Kemi has portrayed this her courageous journey with an engaging, frank and realistic assessment of the highs and lows that come with the period of waiting. It wasn't easy, never is, but Jehovah proved Himself as always, a faithful God.

The word of God will not change. His faithfulness will forever stand on the integrity of His word. I encourage all women still in God's waiting room to be encouraged by Kemi's testimony and be prepared to learn all the Lord wants to teach during this season of waiting.

You will fulfill your purpose. Your wait will not be in vain. Like Kemi, your day of testimony too will come soon, and very soon in Jesus' mighty name. Amen.

Yewande Zaccheaus
Author, God's Waiting Room 1, 2 and 3

Acknowledgements

Firstly, I would like to thank Almighty God for His inspiration to write this book and the opportunity to positively impact lives to hold on to fruitfulness.

I cannot express enough thanks to Ms Ade Adewunmi, who has been a marvellous editor; working with you was very interesting and an extremely rewarding endeavour. My other pair of eyes; Funmilola Faloye, Alison Odubela and Helen Sewell-Canguya, thank you for taking your precious time to proof read, your critical views were well appreciated.

I would have to say that I could not have continued this journey without the boundless support I received from my parents, Mrs. Bridget Adebayo (glad you encouraged me to write this book) and Mr. & Mrs. E K Faloye; your examples of living a prayer filled life and your demonstrations of Faith have been inspiring. Of course, not forgetting the love my husband and I always received from our siblings, showing us constantly, what it means to be part of a great family.

To my mentors and Pastors, it isn't a coincidence that our paths have crossed, definitely ordained from heaven. A big thank you to Pastor Sola & Pastor Bimbo Fola-Alade, Pastor & Mrs. A. Adewumi, Mr. & Mrs. A. Salami, Mr. & Mrs. H. Akuffo, Pastor Banks and Mr. & Dr. (Mrs). A. Adebisi.

A big thank you from the bottom of my heart to esteemed family members and friends for the support you gave my husband and me during our journey. Words cannot express our gratitude. Special thank you also goes to the following guys for meeting my specific demands for your time and love: Ruby Adesuyi, The Otsapas, Isi-buttercup, Adetunjis, The Maks family and my Lighthouse buddies.

Saving the best for last, with special thanks to God Almighty, for my loving husband Seun Faloye, you have been reliable and a strong encourager throughout different seasons in my life. Thank you for your continuous support throughout our marriage; your gentle words and encouragement when I struggled to put words on paper to write my manuscript. Also a big thank you to our son, Theodore-Daniel, you are indeed a testimony of God's faithfulness, thank you for sparing me the time I needed so that I could meet my deadlines to complete this book.

Introduction

This book touches on a common but sensitive topic in our society. It is an issue that has affected many marriages and families regardless of race, creed, and socioeconomic status. Infertility is or has been a cause of heartache for many families, but like other challenges, it can be overcome.

I know from personal experience that the loss of a child – in whatever stage of pregnancy – or difficulty in conceiving can be painful and frustrating. My journey through eleven miscarriages has certainly borne this out. The entire experience was an emotional roller coaster. I can recall times of frustration and anger as I desperately sought answers that simply weren't forthcoming. I remember helpless confusion as I wondered why I was suffering so much for something that I'd always considered to be my right as a woman.

Needless to say, women can be fulfilled whether they are mothers or not. But women who do want children will attest that few things evoke similar longing and desire. I can honestly say that I haven't experienced anything that has hurt as much as a miscarriage. I have heard women who have struggled to conceive say the same thing.

While painfully searching for answers, I became aware that I was not alone in the struggle. I discovered many other people experiencing the same pain, bewilderment, and confusion while holding out for the same hope. I found these people mostly through Internet support forums, which were something of a mixed bag. It was great to draw on the support of others who understood what I was going through and to learn from their experiences, but some of the stories I heard were so harrowing, they just drained me of hope. In writing this book, I hope to offer you more of the former – support and insights into my lived experience. Having survived the tough pain of eleven miscarriages, I want to share my story with you.

I underwent a transformation on my journey to motherhood. I went from being angry, hurt, confused, and uncertain of God's purposes for me to being assured of His love, confident in His purposes for me and in my ability to claim His promises. I arrived at a fresh understanding of the words of Jesus, as recorded in the book of Matthew:

> That is why I tell you not to worry about everyday life – whether you have enough food and drink, or enough clothes to wear. Isn't life more than food, and your body more than clothing? Look at the birds. They don't plant or harvest or store food in barns, for your heavenly Father feeds them. And aren't you far more valuable to him than they are? Can all your worries add a single moment to your life? Matthew 6:25–27 (NLT).

I learned that regardless of what my immediate circumstances might suggest, I am valuable to God, He cares for me, and so I can rest in Him.

I also learned to fight. When I came to the realisation that the two main manifestations of delay when it comes to having children – miscarriages and difficulty in conceiving – are both contrary to God's plan for multiplication and fruitfulness in our lives, I learned to fight for His promises instead. My hope is that I will be able to encourage those facing similar challenges to grasp this awareness of God's purposes, claim what is theirs, and refuse to settle for anything less.

In the book of Romans, the Bible states that 'we know that in all things, God works for the good of those who love him, who have been called according to his purpose,'[1] and this has certainly been my experience. Through heartache and pain, I've emerged emotionally stronger and deeper in my faith. More amazingly, my experiences have provided me with the raw materials to be a blessing to those going through similar challenges who might be feeling isolated, incomplete, or broken. I have felt all those things but have pulled through, and I believe you can too. I hope that this book will help families going through the challenge of infertility to have faith in God's love even as they fight for the fulfilment of His promises. There is light at the end of the tunnel.

---

[1] Romans 8:28 (NIV)

"Life is a gift …..

Life is a test…...

Life is temporary assignment...."

— Rick Warren, *The Purpose Driven Life:*
What on Earth Am I Here for?

CHAPTER 1

The Early Days

I didn't spend a lot of time thinking about marriage and family life as I was growing up. However, when these things did cross my mind, I considered them as no more than part of the natural progression of life. I didn't have outlandish dreams; I was sensible enough to know that the Cinderella story is just a fairy tale. Having said that, I did imagine myself being a good wife to a good husband, raising lovely children, and living in a big mansion. Hey, everyone – even practical and sensible girls like me – has dreams, right? You could say I fully bought into society's definition of success. I did not think about the life challenges that might pop up along the way.

It wasn't that I'd led a particularly charmed life or that things never went wrong. It's just that even when they did, they seemed to sort themselves out to turn out all right in the end. After primary school, I got into a really good secondary school. After that, I was accepted to study law at a well-respected university. I met the man of my dreams a year after law school, and we got married five years later – so far, so average. I don't think my life up to this point was remarkable in any way. In fact, I think many people will be able to relate to my story of a relatively untroubled early life.

I remember when Seun and I were first married. We were so happy and excited about the future. The thought that we might not be able to have children once we decided we were ready to never crossed our minds. It seemed reasonable to expect that when we were ready for children, we would have them. After all, what could be more natural?

Seun and I spent the first two years of our courtship in Nigeria. When an opportunity to study for a postgraduate degree arose in the UK, I emigrated to take the opportunity. The rest of our courtship was long-distance. As a result, after we got married, my husband and I decided to wait for a year before starting a family. He'd gone through the upheaval of relocating to a new country, and we thought it would be best if we gave ourselves some time to settle into and enjoy married life.

One afternoon, exactly a year after our wedding, I felt a sudden and sharp abdominal pain and was rushed to the accident and emergency unit of our local hospital. Tests confirmed that I was pregnant. In a blunt manner that I can only describe as unsympathetic, the gynaecologist informed my husband and me that I had suffered a miscarriage. It felt as if a grenade had been lobbed at us. The shock was amplified because I hadn't even realised I was pregnant!

I got the all-clear and was discharged with the advice not to worry because it was my first pregnancy. I was told that miscarriages of first pregnancies weren't uncommon and was reassured to hear that women who miscarry the first time around usually go on to carry their next pregnancy to full term. We decided that we'd try again later.

I got pregnant without any difficulty after just a couple of months of trying. I was delighted. However, it was not long before I felt the same excruciating pain I'd felt during my first pregnancy. I was rushed to the hospital, where I received the dreadful news – once again, it was all over. My husband and I were crushed. At that point, we had no idea that within the space of eleven months, we would suffer a total of three miscarriages. The hurting had only just begun. We were only starting out on our search for answers to the questions 'Why is this happening?' and 'Why us?'

My husband and I didn't feel we could tell anyone. It felt like something to be ashamed of – and, anyway, how could we burden our friends and families with such sad news? I would stare at myself in the mirror, wondering what was wrong with me. It felt as though we were all alone in the world.

Whenever people playfully hinted that we ought to be thinking of starting a family, I would pretend that we had deliberately chosen not to have children yet, that we wanted to enjoy the honeymoon phase of our marriage a bit longer. Since my pregnancies never advanced to the point where there was a noticeable bump, I could pretend that all was well. Statistics show that one in every seven pregnancies ends in a miscarriage. I was not willing to become another statistic.

Earlier in this chapter, I remarked that many readers can probably relate to my fairly uneventful and relatively trouble-free early life. By the same token, I imagine that many can also relate to the unsettling experience of suddenly struggling and repeatedly failing to reach a normal life milestone. It's unsettling precisely because, up to that point, things had gone fairly smooth. Up to that point, you thought you were good at doing life.

Before getting married and trying to start a family, I did have a few older friends who were trying, unsuccessfully, to have children. I was concerned for them, but I always felt at a loss when it came to comforting them. I prayed for them whenever they came to mind, but I could not relate to their situation at all. Needless to say, I never proffered any advice.

I remember hearing acronyms and words such as *IVF*, *IUI*, *miscarriage*, and *adoption* when people spoke in hushed, sympathetic tones about options for 'waiting couples.' Until I faced this myself, I'd only thought of adoption in terms of something people did after having their own children because they had the financial means to do so and wanted to show love to a child less fortunate than their own. If you're thinking, 'Wow, she sounds naïve,' I would agree with your assessment. I was very naïve, but a lot has happened since then.

They say experience is the best teacher. It's a cliché, but it describes my story perfectly. I am now able to relate to those waiting couples in ways that I could not have dreamed of in those early days.

"Never be afraid to trust an unknown future to a known God."

— <u>Corrie ten Boom</u>

CHAPTER 2

The Start of the Journey of Faith

The hospital gave us no relief in our quest for answers. As a matter of policy, they would not initiate any investigation into the possible causes of recurrent miscarriages until a woman had experienced at least three. I was horrified at the prospect of another miscarriage, and besides, I needed answers right away. I remembered a book I'd heard of several years prior, *Supernatural Childbirth* by Jackie Mize. I got a copy and devoured it.

The book was an eye-opener. I realised that many others had been through similarly harrowing experiences; I was not the only one. I began to feel better, not because others had suffered too, but because they had overcome. I developed a much more positive outlook after reading the book. The worst cases in the book described women who had suffered three miscarriages before having their babies. I reassured myself that my situation couldn't be any worse. It was also comforting to realise that the 'Why me?' question was not unique to me. 'It's not that you're weak,' I'd tell myself. 'After all, other women wondered exactly the same thing while they were going through this challenge.'

However, I learned that while these feelings and questions were normal, I couldn't wallow in them. I had to work on my faith. More specifically, I had to guard my thoughts, and the best way to do that was to focus on the word of God as set out in the Bible. Up until that point, I hadn't really considered the importance of my faith. Instead, I relied on and drew my hope from statistics I found on the Web and in reports of medical research findings. Being armed with facts and figures is good; knowledge can help keep fear at bay. However, I found I needed more than that to keep me going. And as the challenge grew bigger, I found this to be even more the case. It took more than facts and statistics to deal with the emotions that accompany lost pregnancies and the battle to conceive.

I had a third miscarriage in October of 2007; three miscarriages in the space of a year. When the third miscarriage occurred, I cried a lot. And then I cried some more. I felt very, very sorry for myself. I slowly began to slip into a state of constant self-pity. I felt this was a justified response to the agonising experience we were going through.

The Macmillan British English Dictionary defines self-pity as 'the feeling that your situation is worse than other people's and that people should feel sad for you.'[2] That's a pretty accurate description of my state of mind at the time. It was a really negative and disempowering place to be. When you are stuck in self-pity, you not only feel sorry for yourself, but you start to seek to escape into a world of your own.

---

[2] http://www.macmillandictionary.com/dictionary/british/self-pity

I became increasingly selfish. I felt as though I was the only person suffering, or at least that I was suffering more than anyone else. I became pretty much oblivious to my husband's feelings. In hindsight, I think my dismissal of his feelings was made easier by the way those who knew about our problems treated us. In cases of infertility, people tend to focus their sympathy on the woman. She's more likely to be consoled; much less thought is given to the husband and how he might be feeling.

I also felt he wasn't being as proactive as he should be about addressing our problems, and I really resented this. I felt that not only was *I* the only one doing any research to try to find the cause of the miscarriages but that Seun wasn't even being open-minded or duly inquisitive enough about the suggestions I was making. I read many articles about the role healthy diets could play in reducing the risk of miscarriages. Whenever Seun didn't share my excitement, chose not to adopt my suggestions, or refused to discuss the matter further, I would get so hurt and frustrated. I felt that he was not being as supportive as he could be.

This introduced a lot of friction into our marriage, and as a result we would have arguments about the most trivial things. We gradually came to the realisation that if we didn't face our challenge together as a team, it would drive us apart. So my husband suggested we address our constant bickering head-on. This was a bit of a no-brainer, as we were both unhappy about the way things were. We talked about our preferred communication styles and explained the types of behaviour that hurt or confused us.

For example, Seun is a man of few words, whereas I am more of a talker. As a result, I tended to interpret his silence as indifference and felt hurt by it. We agreed that we would have to work harder at accepting one another's differences when it came to communication styles. I had to accept the fact that Seun did not buy into my thinking on diet and fertility, but it didn't mean he was unconcerned about our childlessness. I learned to tell him when I was upset about something and give him the chance to explain, rather than stew in annoyance. Through this, I also learned, Seun was also doing his own researches online and seeking answers through them.

In order to stand a chance at getting through the challenge of infertility, it's important to deal with the issues and tensions that infertility can introduce into the important relationships in your life, primarily your marriage. A close friend shared a similar feeling she experienced through her own challenge of infertility. She recalled the temptation to withdraw socially, and how her husband was both a source of strength and frustration. She reflected:

> Luckily, my husband was my solid rock, and we were a tag team all the way. I took so many things out on him, but he always understood. He always let me cry, vent, or lament. He wasn't perfect, though. He also frustrated me with his stubbornness sometimes. He wasn't always quick to 'cooperate' during my fertile moments, and he'd complain about the lack of spontaneity in our sex life. So we had arguments almost every time I ovulated. Infertility was the hardest journey I ever took.

Self-pity can open the door to suspicion and even paranoia. During this period, I doubted the authenticity of the feelings of those who expressed concern or sorrow about our experiences. 'No one could possibly know what we're going through,' I'd think to myself. Even well-meaning and loving comments were misunderstood if I knew the speaker had never struggled with infertility.

This suspicion was probably fuelled in part by our isolation. We hadn't shared the sad news of the miscarriages with many people. Whatever the contributing factors, the result was hypersensitivity and a lack of graciousness. Self-pity does not leave any room for the attributes of love.

I also found myself struggling with jealousy. At one point, it seemed as though *everyone* I knew was getting pregnant. This is obviously statistically improbable and completely ridiculous, but that's how I felt. I started seeing pregnant women everywhere: on the train to work, at my workplace, at the shopping centre, and in restaurants. I would catch myself staring at these women enviously. 'Why them and not me?' I'd wonder to myself.

There were times when I refused to visit friends or to go to certain places because they triggered an unbearable yearning within me for my own children. I recall conversations I had with my husband in which I would try to get out of going to friends' parties if I thought there might be a couple of pregnant friends present. If I couldn't talk my way out of going and I did bump into these pregnant friends, the car ride back home would be a very quiet one. My mind would be filled with thoughts about the unfairness of life and how I had been left out of the motherhood club.

At first I rationalised my behaviour, but after a while I had to be honest and admit it was good old-fashioned envy. This realisation was something of a jolt. I'd never been given to envy. The awareness came with a sense of condemnation. After all, it isn't a very Christian emotion.

Once I had diagnosed envy, I knew I had to nip it and its symptoms in the bud. Symptoms included being uncomfortable around pregnant women and anger towards God for not giving me a child yet. I decided to adopt a form of exposure therapy and confront my discomfort head-on by engaging expectant mothers in conversation about their experiences of pregnancy and offering to help. For example, I would offer to cook meals so they could put their feet up. Over time, I found their excitement and anticipation of impending motherhood impossible to resist; I was drawn into their joy. My jealousy was gradually replaced by this joy along with the quiet knowledge that these interactions were preparing me for pregnancy and motherhood.

I don't want to pretend that facing up to the character weaknesses my childlessness was revealing was an easy process. The emotional upheaval associated with dealing with these emotions was significant. In fact, just dealing with the knowledge that I was capable of such feelings was draining. Having said that, my advice to anyone fighting these negative emotions is to be ruthless in weeding them out.

Despite the overall benefits of addressing these problems, the process left me feeling very emotionally fragile. Concerned for my mental well-being, my husband insisted that we take a break from trying for a baby and focus on other things. His words were a lifeline, and I gratefully clung to them. I was aware that I was on the verge of sinking into depression, and I was desperate not to. I decided to focus on my career and take a break from trying to have a child. Making the mental shift was very difficult, but it was the only way I knew to cope.

Throwing myself into work anesthetised me from the pain. I buried myself in busyness to distract myself from my worries. Obviously, the underlying issues remained unresolved, but the distraction of work was a respite. Thankfully, my decision to focus on my job coincided with an upswing in my career. My work was interesting and there was much to keep me busy.

Also, as part of my mental shift in gears, I decided to invest more time and effort in my spiritual well-being. I wanted, *needed*, to connect with God so much more. I did this by reading Christian books on having children and handling emotions, listening to sermons on faith, and engaging in regular fellowship with my Bible study group. I was encouraged by words from the Bible with regard to spiritual well-being: 'My dear friend, I pray that everything may go well with you and that you maybe in good health – as I know you are well in spirit.'[3]

This marked the beginning of my journey of faith. Over the course of the next year, I would stumble and fall, but I never quite departed from it. I'm so thankful that I embarked upon it, as it became the driver of my personal transformation, and it sustained me on my rocky road to motherhood.

---

[3] 3 John 1:2 (GNT)

"Faithless is he that says farewell
when the road darkens."

— J.R.R. Tolkien

CHAPTER 3

Entering the Valley of Shocks

After a break of about seven months, we decided to try again. We were no longer frazzled, and while the pain of our past losses hadn't disappeared, it was much less acute. We were positive that all would be well this time round.

By this point, we were no longer living in London. We had moved to Essex, and I loved our new and bigger home. The only downside was that we weren't able to begin the tests that would help the doctors determine the cause of past miscarriages right away. This was because my new local hospital had not yet received my medical records.

The delay didn't cause me to lose hope. I felt we were ready to begin trying again, so we did. And then I got the first body blow: another miscarriage. In fact, over a period of eight months, my husband and I suffered three more miscarriages. This brought the tally of lost pregnancies to six.

During this same eight-month period, the doctors started a battery of tests to try to determine the cause of the problem. My husband and I were tested, and the results showed us both to be in perfect health. Doctors could find absolutely nothing wrong. There didn't seem to be a medical explanation for my six miscarriages. If we were both fine, why did I keep miscarrying? I was really disheartened, because most of the cases of recurrent miscarriages that I'd read about as part of my online research could be traced to specific causes.

Also, like many people living in our modern world of almost relentless scientific breakthrough, I have come to expect that problems should have solutions. The lack of answers was unbearable. I needed to know why this was happening to me. With growing desperation, I trawled the Internet for answers. I spent hours poring over the research behind the purported benefits of various natural remedies. I hunted for stories of medical professionals in other parts of the world who were trialling innovative new treatments that were yielding results. None of this was to any avail, but I became addicted to the process regardless.

This messy situation really tested my faith. I mean faith in the biblical sense, 'the confidence that what we hope for will actually happen; [and which] ... gives us assurance about things we cannot see.'[4] I read and understood the promises with regard to having children as set out in the Bible but couldn't understand why they didn't seem to be at work in my own life. Promises such as, 'Behold, children are a heritage from the Lord, the fruit of the womb is a reward. Like arrows in the hand of a warrior, so are the children of one's youth' from the book of Psalms[5] and 'there

---

4   Hebrews 11:1 (NLT)

5   Psalm 127:3–4 (NKJV)

will be no miscarriages or infertility in your land, and I will give you long, full lives' from the book of Exodus[6].

I knew I had to keep believing the promises of God with regard to parenthood, but it was proving difficult. Fear crept into my heart. Whenever I tried to draw strength from those promises, the memories of my past losses would bubble up. If, as they say, fear is the opposite of faith, then I was failing this test of faith. And without faith, how can one be hopeful?

Aside from the issue of fear, I had to deal with my anger. I can remember a time after the fifth loss when I got so angry about the situation. I was angry about the pain, angry that my joy was being cut short, but most of all I was actually angry with God. I felt like I had been taken to the top of a cliff and pushed off. I did not feel like praying or reading the Bible or hearing any words of comfort. In the heat of the moment, it felt like the anger would last forever.

I stewed in my anger for days. I refused to pray or read my Bible, nor was I moved by the words or Bible-verse quotations from my husband and others in this regard. However, the lyrics of the various worship and praise songs that Seun played reminded me of God's love in a way that I couldn't deny.

Time, they say, heals all, but it wasn't time that healed my relationship with God. The reality was that I couldn't get away from the truth of His goodness. I chose to trust what I knew of Him. I wasn't sure how I was going to get through what I was facing, but I couldn't think of a better source of help or support for the journey. I simply could not turn my back on His words of love and His promises of faithfulness.

---

[6] Exodus 23:26 (NLT)

In the midst of this very dark period, after one of the miscarriages, I went to see one of my church pastors for advice. In addition to praying with me, she introduced me to a lady to whom, over time, I became very close. This lady became a mentor as well as a friend. She had experienced twelve miscarriages before giving birth to two beautiful children. As she shared her experiences with me, I felt understood, and I was able to open up about my struggle with self-pity and prayerlessness. Being able to acknowledge and confront these things was the first step in the journey to becoming strong enough to remain hopeful in the face of the bigger challenge I was facing.

Through our conversations, I learned that success in life doesn't hinge on a single challenge, however big. Rather, it depends on how we respond to the series of challenges that we encounter in life. Giving up hope in the face of the first big obstacle is a recipe for getting nowhere. This is a truth that has been borne out on my journey towards motherhood; you've just got to keep going. The more time I spent with my new friend and mentor, the more I learned about holding on to faith no matter what you are faced with.

When she shared the many challenges she went through – twelve miscarriages, marital issues, and the isolation that followed – they seemed to me to be too much for one person to bear. She explained that while it might appear that she struggled all alone, the reality was that God had been her constant companion throughout her journey. It was during that period that she learned the importance of constant communication with Him. She learned to pray without giving up.

My mentor drew my attention to a verse in the Bible that said 'never stop praying.'[7] She encouraged me to turn my tears and painful emotions into heartfelt prayers to God. This required me to focus less on my circumstances and more on God in worship and prayer. As difficult as this was, I began to realise that as long as I could trust God and maintain my resolve, I would see the end of this challenge.

My regular telephone conversations, visits, and emails with my mentor were very uplifting. She had many encouraging words for me. She shared scriptures on faith that she advised me to meditate on regularly, but just as importantly she was generally fun to hang out with. Every encounter with her left me feeling refreshed, energised, and ready to take on the world.

I didn't acquire this new perspective immediately. My story isn't about the power of positive thinking; it's much bigger than that. Months went by, and my hopes and wishes for a child of my own remained unfulfilled, but I was learning the secrets of faith and hope. I held out. I would say to myself, 'So nothing happened this month. Maybe it will happen next month or even next year. It will happen, because God has said so. I'm not giving up.'

Self-examination played an important role in my efforts to grow my faith. For example, it helped me to realise that I had allowed bitterness and being unforgiving to flourish in my heart. I knew these negative emotions had no place in my life if I wanted to be filled with faith. Besides, I wouldn't want any future child of mine growing up in a home with such unproductive emotions.

---

[7] 1 Thessalonians 5:17 (ERV)

Bitterness and unforgivingness often stem from unresolved or poorly resolved offence. Learning how to forestall offence or deal with it in a healthy way is vital to addressing bitterness and unforgivingness. Emotionally difficult situations like long-term infertility are often ripe for misunderstanding and offence.

People behave in different ways when they become aware that you are dealing with an intractable problem like infertility. Some, in a bid to show sympathy, are quick to inform you that they 'know exactly what you're going through.' This is despite the fact that they have never had a problem conceiving or lost a pregnancy or a baby. Others are quick to offer their opinions on the cause of the problem and advice on what you should do to overcome it. I remember one tactless but well-meaning friend who told me that my husband and I were experiencing repeated miscarriages because we were slow to learn the lesson that God was trying to teach us. She advised me to pick up the pace of our learning! Much of this advice was given with good intentions, but it ended up hurting rather than helping.

Some people will let you know that you are in their thoughts in a bid to reassure you that you're not alone. Although it's nice to know that others are thinking of you during a difficult period, I really wished fewer people felt the need to inform me of this fact. I would have appreciated their silent prayers a lot more.

Being on the receiving end of so much advice and so many opinions can be exhausting. My husband and I began to find it a little too much to handle. In this state, it was easy to take offence where none was intended or to respond in ways that left others feeling hurt or unappreciated. We had to learn to firmly but politely refuse the advice of those who did not understand what we were going through. This approach didn't always work, so we also had to get really good at avoiding extended conversations with some people. In this way, I protected my mind and reduced opportunities for offence and bitterness. This process is harder in some societies and cultures than others. A Nigerian friend who lives in Lagos found the stigma associated with infertility particularly hard to deal with.

Not all my bitterness was the result of other people's insensitivity. I can think of one situation, involving an acquaintance, when my bitterness was caused by my decision to revel in self-pity. It is important to recognise the difference between hypersensitivity borne of self-pity and the legitimate hurt caused by the tactless comments of other people.

This acquaintance got married and after a few years became pregnant. She excitedly shared this piece of news. Her prayers had finally been answered! On the face of it, I was glad for her, but on a deeper level I had to admit that all was not well with me. I noticed that I didn't want to be around her. Out of nowhere, I began to get flashbacks to a disagreement we'd had some years before for which she'd never apologised. The intensity of the resentment I still felt startled me. I used this lack of a formal apology to justify my being unforgiving. She had treated me badly in the past, and yet here she was enjoying a blessing that I desperately desired. Life was so unfair! I thought I had forgiven any offence and moved on, but I obviously hadn't, and self-pity had opened up old wounds.

Once I had diagnosed being unforgiving, I knew I had to confront it. I had to make a choice about what was more important to me, forgiveness and the freedom and happiness it brings, or unforgivingness and my empty self-righteousness. I chose the former. There was no angelic intervention or voice from heaven; it was an act of will. My acquaintance and I are now on cordial terms, but things were strained for a while.

The Bible tells us that being unforgiving is a negative emotion that does no good and allows the devil to get the upper hand over us by opening up the door to other negative emotions that rob us of our peace. The Apostle Paul advised Christians to guard against it, 'for when I forgive, if indeed I need to forgive anything – I do it in Christ's presence because of you, in order to keep Satan from getting the upper hand over us; for we know what his plans are.'[8]

Just as importantly, forgiving others is a requirement for God's forgiveness. So much so that Jesus taught us to pray, 'forgive us our debts, as we also have forgiven our debtors.'[9] This is a hard principle to live by when we're hurting as a result of the actions of others – for example, a betrayal by a spouse or friend or abuse at the hands of a relative. I do not pretend to be an expert on dealing with the pain that accompanies such traumatic events. However, my advice in such cases would be to seek appropriate help as soon as possible in order to offload the additional weight of being unforgiving.

---

[8] 2 Corinthians 2:10–11 (GNT)

[9] Matthew 6:12 (NIV)

"Only in the darkness can you see the stars."

— <u>Martin Luther King Jr.</u>

CHAPTER 4

The Power of Knowledge:
Knowing Your God ...
and Knowing Your Enemy!

We experienced our seventh miscarriage in the middle of 2009. My local hospital referred us to a specialist at the Recurrent Miscarriage Clinic (RMC) in London. The doctors believed the clinic would be able to carry out diagnostic tests that they were unable to. Eight weeks after the referral was made, we got an appointment at the clinic.

I had done some research into the clinic, and I knew it had an impressive track record. I searched online forums for reviews from couples who had received treatment there. I read articles about the cutting-edge research conducted by the clinic's medical team. All the articles and reviews highlighted the comprehensive work of the dedicated medical staff as they sought to find the causes of patients' miscarriages. The facilities were also impressive, and I was excited and hopeful. My hope was anchored not only in medical science but also in my belief that God gives medical scientists the wisdom to carry out research and find solutions to medical problems.

Ahead of the appointment, we were given a document outlining the various diagnostic tests the specialist would be conducting over a six-week period. Following a short consultation, the tests began. They revealed that I had an autoimmune disorder called anti-phospholipid syndrome, which is a blood-clotting condition. Essentially, the blood clots and restricts blood flow to the placenta. As a result, the foetus does not receive sufficient blood supply. This was the likely cause of the recurrent miscarriages. Apart from the risk of this condition to the baby, there is also a potential risk to the health of the mother, which can lead to a stroke or some other debilitating condition.

A further appointment with the consultant was scheduled to discuss the condition and the course of treatments that would be necessary for a successful pregnancy. I went into researcher mode once again. Prior to this appointment to discuss the diagnosis, I spent countless hours researching the condition on the Internet. I wanted to have a good idea of what we were up against, but in simple terms. I was determined not to let the big medical terms being flung about intimidate me or open the door to fear. I had learned enough on my spiritual journey to know that fear opposes faith.

By the time my husband and I sat down with the consultant, I was armed with plenty of information and had prepared my questions. The result was a fruitful discussion. The consultant answered all my questions and clarified the aspects of the treatment that I was struggling to understand. My preparation was certainly important for protecting my mental and spiritual well-being, but I like to think it made the consultant's job easier, if only because he didn't have a terrified mess of a woman on his hands!

A friend of mine who also struggled with infertility told me of the comfort that she derived from being well informed. Her infertility was caused by blocked fallopian tubes and compounded by adhesions (internal scars that are made up of strand-like fibrous tissues forming abnormal bridges/bonds between two parts of the body after trauma such as surgery) from a surgical procedure, known as a myomectomy, to remove fibroids that were growing in her womb. She recalls becoming so well informed that her doctor used to joke that she made him feel redundant.

In my case, it was such a relief to finally have a diagnosis. For so long we had been battling shadows; now we knew what we were fighting. This didn't change the *way* I fought the spiritual battle, but it did remove some of the mystique that had surrounded the challenge. Once things became less mysterious, they also became a lot less intimidating. In other words, things took on their proper proportion – and in comparison to God's greatness, every challenge is small.

I think knowledge-gathering is essential when facing any problem. Think about it: If you were a general tasked with leading your country's army into war against an enemy, you'd gather as much information as you could about your opponents. You'd use this information to develop your military strategy. Once anti-phosphilipid syndrome was determined to be the cause of the miscarriages and I had learned as much as I could about the condition, I knew my enemy.

My spiritual 'military strategy' included focused daily prayer about the medical condition. Also, during the day, I would speak words of faith to my body. I would say things like, 'My blood will clot normally during pregnancy by the power of God, in the name of Jesus.' As a believer of God's Word, I had an assurance that I could go to my Almighty Father in prayer and ask Him to cause my blood to clot properly.

My detailed knowledge of the condition helped me to make my prayer requests very specific. It also helped to drive out fear and anger. As a result, my prayer time was calmer and so much more refreshing. This clarity of mind was obviously for my benefit. God is able to answer prayers whether they are focused or not. I often tell people that even a bad medical report needn't cause fear. It can bring you to a place of knowledge and help you direct your prayers more intelligently.

Following the diagnosis, I was prescribed small doses of aspirin tablets and blood-thinning injections, which I had to take from the time a pregnancy was confirmed until the baby was born. To say that injecting myself with a blood thinner every day throughout the course of the pregnancy did not fill me with enthusiasm is something of an understatement. My husband was even less pleased at the prospect of our being tied to an unnatural and uncomfortable process. He believed that having gone through so much pain already, we shouldn't have to deal with the discomfort of self-administered daily injections.

I could see his point – and as I explained earlier, I wasn't thrilled with the idea of daily injections. To be honest, I hate the fuss associated with taking any medications. When I'm ill, I often forget to take them. To make matters worse, I'm a bit scared of needles. Whenever I have to travel abroad and I need to get vaccinated, I'm always a little frightened.

However, I decided I was going take the blood-thinning injections while praying to God to heal me. Besides, it wasn't as though I would have to take them forever; it was just for the duration of the pregnancy. If this was what it would take to have our child, then I would get over my fear of needles and dislike of medication. You see, I have always believed that the discoveries of science have been made through the wisdom of God. I genuinely don't see a conflict between medical treatment and faith.

A month later, I became pregnant again, and I was thrilled. I got in touch with the early pregnancy unit so that I could pick up my prescription slip for the blood-thinning injections. Also, as I'd never self-administered injections before, it was necessary for a nurse to show me how to do so.

The hospital arranged for me to have an ultrasound scan to ensure everything was proceeding normally. The scan showed that my baby had a heartbeat and was growing at the expected rate. I was diligent about taking the medication daily. I didn't miss a single injection or aspirin tablet. That isn't to suggest I enjoyed the process. It took several minutes and a lot of psyching myself up before I could bring myself to inject my abdomen.

Despite my diligence, about three weeks later I started bleeding and lost my eighth pregnancy. I remember thinking to myself, 'This is not supposed to be happening.' The specialists at the clinic had said the blood-clotting condition was treatable and they had a high success rate of doing just that. I put the eighth loss down to not commencing my treatment early enough. I made up my mind that next time, I would request that the clinic administer treatment at an earlier point. I was hurt and disappointed, but I wasn't crushed.

After the loss, I was booked in for an ultrasound scan in order to check that my uterus was clear of the failed pregnancy. In other words, the doctors wanted to be sure that the miscarriage had been complete and there was nothing that could cause complications in later pregnancies. Later, when I met with the consultant, I followed through on my resolution regarding demanding an earlier commencement of treatment. I requested that my general practitioner (GP) be allowed to prescribe the medication so I could start treatment as soon as I became pregnant. This would remove the need for me to arrange to see my consultant at the clinic. I explained that I was eager to avoid any delay in the process.

The consultant felt this was a sensible approach, and a letter was duly sent to my GP. The consultant also made the decision to increase the dosage of the blood-thinning injections.

I was anxious to get pregnant again, but because I'd experienced some bleeding post-miscarriage, I decided to wait for at least two menstrual cycles before trying. Once I was sure, through a home pregnancy test, that I was pregnant for the ninth time, I wasted no time in calling my GP. I arranged to pick up my prescription on the same day and commenced treatment immediately. I also booked an appointment at the clinic. An ultrasound scan was carried out, and it showed that the pregnancy was going well.

However, a few days later I began to bleed. A further scan showed bleeding in the womb, but the consultants explained that this was a sub-chronic hematoma (blood clot in the uterus). These sorts of clots could and often did dissolve as a pregnancy progressed. Despite these assurances, I lost the ninth pregnancy.

I began to wonder and question my faith. I had prayed and believed in the word of God. The more I thought about it, the more bewildered I became. Looking back, I can see that I was in deep shock. At the time I just felt emotionally numb. All I had were my questions, and they would continually race through my mind.

This had a knock-on effect on my prayer life. I didn't stop praying, but the *way* I prayed changed. I didn't want to go through the rigmarole of conventional prayer. I didn't want to talk *at* God, I wanted to talk *to* Him. And more importantly, I wanted Him to talk back. I needed to understand what was going on. And He was the only one whose answers I hadn't really heard yet.

I wondered what else I had to do in order to receive the blessing of a child. I was exhausted. All the discomfort of injecting myself with the medication had been for nothing. I wondered how much more I could take. Also, due to the economic recession, my plans to break into a new area of legal practice were being frustrated. I was experiencing an extended season of unsuitable and unrewarding employment, so I was unable to bury myself in my work.

I found myself questioning the truth of a familiar Bible verse: 'No test or temptation that comes your way is beyond the course of what others have had to face. All you need to remember is that

God will never let you down; he'll never let you be pushed past your limit; he'll always be there to help you come through it.'[10] I felt this test was definitely too much for me to bear and that I was being pushed beyond the limits of what I could handle.

I turned my prayer time into extended conversations with God in which I would express my pain at not being able to see any light at the end of the tunnel and then ask for His strength to help me carry on. During these times, I would receive assurances from God through the Bible. A passage from the book of Hebrews was particularly helpful: 'Since God assured us, 'I'll never let you down, never walk off and leave you,' we can boldly quote, God is there, ready to help; I'm fearless no matter what. Who or what can get to me?'[11]

These biblical assurances from God were a lifeline. They weren't new to me, but I found myself reading them with fresh eyes and receiving a new understanding about them. Also, my mentor told me about a church support group for couples who were looking to God for children. My husband and I became regular attendees at group meetings. We met with other couples who were struggling to have children, and we prayed together and drew strength from the testimonies of those who had received their miracle babies. These gatherings were like fuel to our faith. It was also a relief not to have to explain how we were feeling, as everyone there was going through or had been through similar challenges and could empathise.

---

[10] 1 Corinthians 10:13 (MSG)

[11] Hebrews 10:5b–6a (MSG)

Despite the fact that I did not yet have what I wanted, I decided not to give in to self-pity but to persevere. My mentor was a consistent source of encouragement. She helped me see how what I was going through would enable me to support couples with similar challenges. If I was able to hold on, then I could encourage them to do the same.

"Pain is the fuel of passion — it energizes us with an intensity to change that we don't normally possess."
— <u>Zondervan Publishing</u>, <u>*The Purpose Driven Life: What on Earth Am I Here For?*</u>

CHAPTER 5

Training for the Fight

In spite of all that had happened, hope wasn't lost. We continued to believe that we'd get a breakthrough. The consultants decided to increase the dosage of my aspirin tablets and other blood-thinning agents after the ninth pregnancy loss. After the loss of the ninth pregnancy, a scripture from the book of James took on a new significance for me:

> Take the old prophets as your mentors. They put up
> with anything, went through everything, and never
> once quit, all the time honoring God. What a gift
> life is to those who stay the course! You've heard,
> of course, of Job's staying power, and you know
> how God brought it all together for him at the end.
> That's because God cares, cares right down to the
> last detail. James 5:10–11 (The Message)

It's not that I considered my challenges to be equivalent to Job's. The Bible describes Job as a man who lost everything – his wealth, children, and health. Despite the extremity of his suffering, he refused to turn his back on God. Through his losses and pain, he chose to honour God. In the past, in the midst of my losses, I would often ask, 'Why me, Lord?' But as my relationship with God evolved, I no longer felt the need to ask such questions. Instead, I learned to ask, 'What do I need to do, Lord?'

I had become increasingly confident in the knowledge that God takes an active interest in every detail of my life. I knew He was fully aware of my situation and that as long as I had life there was hope. I drew a lot of encouragement from meditating on that Bible verse from the book of James. I did not get a direct answer as to why I was facing these challenges (and I still haven't), but my focus shifted from wanting to know why things were happening to wanting to know how to overcome them.

Recognising that life-disrupting challenges were not unique to me and that people like Job had survived much worse helped to focus my mind. Job's story helped me understand that even the worst challenges don't last forever. We just need to hang on long enough to see them come to an end. This realisation was not immediate or automatic. I came to it over a long and painful period of time, and it took a conscious effort to believe God's promises, as set out in the Bible, about fruitfulness and children.

This new confidence was buoyed by a supernatural affirmation of my faith in the form of a prophecy. A visiting pastor confirmed my expectation of the gift of a child from God. He prophesied that God had heard my prayers and that my husband and I needed to pray against losing my pregnancy. At the time, I was a few weeks into the tenth pregnancy. I had never received a public prophecy before, but I believed it because it seemed to confirm a dream my husband had a few days before. In my husband's dream, a particular month featured very prominently. Neither of us was able to decipher the significance of the month. However, the very same date was mentioned in the prophecy. The pastor explained that there was spiritual opposition to the birth of the child and that on the date he had mentioned there would be a concerted spiritual attack against my pregnancy. He emphasised the importance of praying against the attack.

To be honest, talk of spiritual attacks made me uncomfortable. Perhaps that was why Seun and I chose not to think too much about it. We just took the prophecy as confirmation that God had heard us, and that was the end of the matter as far as we were concerned. Looking back, I'm amazed at how nonchalant we were and how little we had studied biblical precedent on spiritual opposition. For example, spiritual opposition played a significant role in the story of Daniel. The Bible records the words of the angel who appeared to Daniel:

> Then he said, 'Don't be afraid, Daniel. Since the first day you began to pray for understanding and to humble yourself before your God, your request has been heard in heaven. I have come in answer to your prayer. But for twenty-one days the spirit prince of the kingdom of Persia blocked my way. Then Michael, one of the archangels, came to help me, and I left him there with the spirit prince of the kingdom of Persia.' Daniel 10:12–13 (NLT).

Daniel had prayed to God for understanding concerning a vision. As explained in the verse above, Daniel's prayers were answered on the day he made them. However, the angel entrusted with delivering the answer to his prayer faced spiritual opposition and was unable to complete his assignment until a stronger angel came to his assistance. The lesson here is that we should *expect* spiritual opposition. At the very least, we shouldn't be surprised by it. It is neither new nor strange.

The prophetic word was both a warning and a confirmation. It clarified the significance of the date that my husband had seen in his dream, and it confirmed that God was not unaware of our faith, nor had He forgotten us. He cared about me and my family. We were convinced that our prayers had been answered.

I was full of relief and gratitude at the prospect of an end to the series of pregnancy losses. My church was praying for me, so I reasoned it was just a matter of time before we would have our baby. As I have already mentioned, I had commenced treatment with the increased dosage of blood-thinning injections as prescribed by my consultant. My last ultrasound had revealed the pregnancy was growing well. It was all blue skies; everything was wonderful. We did not give further thought to the warning about spiritual opposition.

The following week, I started bleeding heavily while experiencing painful stomach cramps. My initial feeling was one of confusion. How could this be happening? I was not expecting this. I felt trapped in a nightmare. I went to the emergency early pregnancy unit of my local hospital. Within a few hours, the medical staff confirmed that the worst had happened – the pregnancy was lost. Another baby I'd never hold.

I was devastated, but something had changed. I was hurting, but my response to the pain was different. Rather than giving in to the emotions of fear, pain, and panic that were crowding in on me, I telephoned my mentor. When I told her the news, I could sense her shock and pain, but she recovered quickly and comforted me.

I knew I had to keep going, but the way forward was fuzzy. I could not understand how this could have happened after I had received a prophetic word, been prayed for continuously by members of my church, and followed an improved treatment regime. In this state of mind, I couldn't handle visitors or phone calls from concerned friends and family members. I only had room for my own bewilderment, disappointment, and confusion; I couldn't cope with anyone else's. I switched off my phone and went to stay with a close friend in Kent, which is about twenty-six miles from my home. I was struggling to understand how I could have received a word from God about an imminent blessing and then lose it. I tried to recall any biblical precedent for this, but I simply couldn't. Everything that came to mind seemed to highlight how strange my experience was.

For example, I remembered the story of a prophecy given to a man and his wife described in the book of Judges.[12] The story was about a man called Manoah whose wife was visited by an angel who told her that she and her husband would have a son. Despite the fact that they had not been able to have children in the past, she was going to become pregnant. The chapter goes on to tell of Manoah's wife giving birth to a son she named Samson.

In addition to the pain from the seeming abnormality of my situation, there was the additional burden of the weight of

---

[12] Judges 13

expectation of my church. The prophetic word was given very publicly. My husband and I had shared the details of our challenges in this area with only a few of our church members. By the next church service, everyone at church knew. Their response to the news of our challenge was love-filled. People began praying for us and giving us words of encouragement. However, there was also so much collective hope.

You might read this and think, 'What's wrong with hope? You should have been grateful that people were so supportive.' I was, but as the Bible says, 'hope deferred makes the heart sick,[13]' and where there is much unfulfilled hope, there is much heart sickness. I couldn't face the disappointment of so many people, nor did I relish the thought of having to explain what had happened to several people. I was unable to face going to church. In the past when we had lost pregnancies, only a few people had known about it. I had been able to smile in public and weep in private. Now there was nowhere to hide.

I balked at the prospect of having to deal with the curious questions, the shock, the pity, and the pain of my fellow church members. I decided to put it out of my mind; I'd cross that bridge when I came to it. In the meantime, I had more pressing matters to attend to, such as getting to the bottom of what had happened. How did we end up here?

As I mentioned earlier, all the biblical precedents that came to mind were those in which men and women received a divine visitation (often by an angel of God) promising them victory or a blessing along with some guidance or instructions. Provided they

---

[13] Proverbs 13:12 (NKJV)

believed the prophecy and followed the guidance or instructions, they would receive everything they were promised. For example, the first chapter of the book of Luke tells the story of the birth of John the Baptist. John's father, Zechariah, was a priest, and one day while he was performing his priestly duties, an angel appeared to him and announced that his wife, Elizabeth, would give birth to a son. This was despite the fact that both Zechariah and Elizabeth were well advanced in age and had never had children.

Granted, I hadn't experienced an angelic visitation, but I *did* receive a prophetic word, and as far as I was aware, I hadn't disregarded any instructions or guidance. So what went wrong? My confidence in the prophetic word stemmed from the fact that it essentially confirmed what we believed God had already revealed to my husband in his dream. Seun was as confused as I was and just as desperate to get some answers. My faith in God was very important in my everyday life. And while I did not fully understand how the gift of prophecy applied to Christians in general, I had a more confident grasp of the centrality of faith in the Christian walk.

I was encouraged by the story of Abraham, to whom God promised a son at the age of seventy-five. Abraham had to wait for twenty-five years to see the fulfilment of that promise. His son, Isaac, wasn't born until Abraham was one hundred years old. As the Bible verse in the book of Numbers states, 'God is not a man, so he does not lie. He is not human, so he does not change his mind. Has he ever spoken and failed to act? Has he ever promised and not carried it through?'[14]

---

[14] Numbers 23:19 (NLT)

This provided me with an assurance that there was no mistake in God's word. I was not immediately comforted, but as they say, time is a healer. Also, one of the pastors at my church had stayed in touch with me through telephone calls and text messages. Her encouragement and advice helped me to see that the fellowship of my church family would guide and help me not fall prey to unproductive thoughts. After a month-long absence, I decided to return to church. At about the same time, my husband and I agreed that we needed to develop a deeper understanding of the prophetic.

"When you're at the end of your rope,
tie a knot and hold on"
— <u>Theodore Roosevelt</u>

CHAPTER 6

A Renewed Hope: Putting Up a Good Fight

After the tenth miscarriage, the chief consultant at the clinic advised us that the best way forward was to perform a laparoscopy on my womb. This would help the medical team ascertain whether the lining of my womb was able to support a baby. This was more intrusive than the X-ray I'd had previously, but it would provide them with better information. The X-ray hadn't revealed any problems with my womb, so the doctors weren't unduly worried.

I did not like the idea of surgery, especially as it would be under general anaesthetic and so I would be unconscious. However, given that my body wasn't responding to the treatment for the anti-phosphilipid syndrome even at the increased dosage, I agreed to the surgery. An appointment was scheduled.

As the date for the surgery drew closer I grew increasingly anxious, but we had gone through so much already I couldn't give up now. Also, I drew strength from the Bible verse I mentioned earlier, that God cares right down to the last detail.[15] I chose to

---

[15] James 5:11(MSG)

continue trusting God and allow the doctors to do all they could to help me.

The surgery was successful, and I was informed that the lining of my womb was in perfect condition. The chief consultant confidently predicted that my next pregnancy would be a smooth one, as the condition of my womb was good to carry babies. She advised me to go ahead and try once more. During this period I had told myself that I would continue to hold on to the promises of God. I kept reading various Bible verses that told of God's desire to bless His people with children; I continued to pray and hold onto these promises every day.

In the meantime, I planned baby showers for friends. I love planning events anyway, so when opportunities arose to put my organisational skills to good use, I took them. This was also an act of faith. I believed that just as I celebrated with friends who were having babies, they would one day celebrate with me. Being surrounded by the joy of new births while holding onto God's promises brought healing to my pain and hurt.

Then I found out I was pregnant again, just a month after the surgery. I was filled with conflicting emotions. Was this one the one? Should I allow myself to get excited? This was my eleventh pregnancy. I can still remember my quiet prayer on finding out I was pregnant: 'Lord, let this be it. No more losses.' By now, I knew the drill by heart, so I wasted no time setting things in motion. I contacted my GP to get a prescription for the blood-thinning injections and telephoned the Early Pregnancy Clinic for an appointment. I was back on the roundabout of activity.

Early scans showed the pregnancy was progressing as expected. There was no bleeding, and I felt fine. I passed the eighth week

– which was the point at which I usually suffered symptoms like bleeding that indicated things were awry – without incident. I was so thankful. I mentioned to the sonographer at the clinic that I was excited to see this pregnancy advance a little bit further than any of the earlier ones. It was great news for my husband and me; even the consultant was quietly optimistic.

After my hospital appointment, I walked back to work, which was about ten minutes away from the clinic. Later that day, on my way home from work, I started experiencing severe stomach cramps. I called my husband and told him about the cramps. He decided he would come home straight away. I asked him to pray with me over the phone because I was beginning to feel faint. My mind was whirring. 'How could this be happening again? Not this time. How could this be happening again?' I thought to myself.

I hurried home, took some painkillers, and tried to pray, but I was in so much pain I found it impossible to focus. I phoned a doctor friend of mine who lived a few miles away and described my symptoms. She advised me to call for an ambulance. I called my husband, who was already on his way home and was very close, and asked him to call the emergency services and let them in. I was in so much pain, and I knew that I would not be able to open the door.

After making the call, I crawled from our bedroom to the bathroom. I had started bleeding heavily. My body went into shock, and I started shivering. My husband and the paramedics arrived a few minutes later, and I was given air and gas to help relieve the pain. I was hurriedly transported into the ambulance to the hospital, sirens wailing all the way. Later that evening, I lost the baby.

This loss was more shocking because it was so sudden. During previous pregnancies, there were warning signs. For example, I would bleed intermittently for about three to four weeks. When I informed my consultant at the clinic about the miscarriage, he was as surprised as we were.

At this point, I no longer had tears to shed. I think bewilderment muted our grief a bit. My husband and I were more interested in understanding what to do next. This loss just didn't make any sense to us; everything about this pregnancy had seemed perfect. We prayed for wisdom. During this period of seeking out answers, we heard a sermon in church about the importance of not treating a prophetic word as a foregone conclusion. My pastor emphasised the importance of prayerfully 'birthing' prophecies. Around the same time, I stumbled upon a Bible scripture that deepened my understanding about words of prophecy: 'This charge I commit to you, son Timothy, according to the prophecies previously made concerning you, that by them you may wage the good warfare.'[16]

This scripture highlighted the role prophecy can play in revealing spiritual opposition. Coupled with the recent church sermon, it was enough to trigger a transformation of my thinking in this area. This new understanding with regard to spiritual warfare had an impact on my prayer time. I began to pray in more varied ways: from petition, thanksgiving, and declaration of Bible verses concerning having children and faith to songs of praise and worship. During this time, I dug up my notes I had made about revelations I had received while reading my Bible over the years, and I recorded new musings about Bible verses I was reading and

---

[16] 1 Timothy 1:18 (NKJV)

researching. I would meditate on these notes during my daily prayer time, and in this way I found fresh inspiration to converse with God.

Prayer and praise were powerful weapons in my fight. The Merriam-Webster dictionary defines prayer as 'an address or petition to God in word or thought[17].'Also in the American English Oxford dictionaries, prayer is described as 'a solemn request for help or expression of thanks addressed to God or an object of worship.'[18] I believe both definitions are accurate.

The Bible encourages us to pray: 'Pray continually, give thanks in all circumstances; for this is God's will for you in Christ Jesus.'[19] The only way I have found to sustain this level of prayer is to believe something else the Bible says: 'And whatever you ask for in prayer, having faith and [really] believing, you will receive.'[20] After all, what's the point of praying to God if you don't really believe you are going to receive what you are asking for?

At the risk of sounding like a broken record, I have to say this didn't happen automatically. There was a time when I prayed for a believing heart. But once there was faith, the rest was easy. I prayed constantly not just about having children but for the future of these children too. I prayed for the wisdom and strength to be a good parent. I prayed that my husband and I wouldn't pass on our negative character traits to our (as yet unborn) children.

---

[17] http://www.merriam-webster.com/dictionary/prayer

[18] http://www.oxforddictionaries.com/us/definition/american_english/prayer

[19] 1 Thessalonians 5:17–18 (NIV)

[20] Matthew 21:22 (AMP)

Constant prayer required me to be flexible and creative about when, where, and how I prayed. I prayed in the early hours of the morning as well as late at night; I prayed during my coffee breaks, bathroom breaks, and on my journey into work. If you're stumped by the prospect of fitting more prayer into your already busy schedule, my advice is that you incorporate prayer into your existing routines. Use these prayer moments as opportunities to pour out the pain you're feeling, your tears, or whatever else you might be feeling to God.

Pouring out one's heart to God in prayer is neither new nor radical. There is biblical precedent. The Bible records the story of a woman called Hannah. She was married to Elkanah and was one of his two wives. Peninnah, the other wife, had children but Hannah had none. Several times a year, the family would travel to the city of Shiloh to observe their religious obligations. Shiloh was the religious capital of Israel before the first temple was built in Jerusalem.

At the time, Israelites living in Judah would assemble in Shiloh for the *Shalosh Regalim*, the three major Jewish pilgrimage festivals: Pesach (Passover), Shavuot (Weeks), and Sukkot (Tents or Booths). Pilgrims would offer sacrifices as a mark of thanksgiving and atonement. People would make sacrifices for themselves and on behalf of their children, and Peninnah would take the opportunity to remind Hannah of her childlessness.

For the sacrifices, Elkannah would give portions of meat to Peninnah and each of her children. As an expression of his love, he would give Hannah an especially generous portion, since she could not receive any additional portions on behalf of her children. Hannah's sadness would cause her to weep and lose her appetite. Elkanah would try to placate her by assuring her that the fact that they didn't have children together didn't make him love her any less. I'm sure most women can understand why these words failed to comfort Hannah. After all, despite his declarations of love, he had married and had children with someone else!

Anyway, during one of these trips, something shifted in Hannah's mind, and she decided to do something other than weep and complain to her husband (and receive more of his 'comforting' words). She cried out to God in prayer instead. The Bible describes Hannah's prayer time in the following way: 'And she was in bitterness of soul, and prayed to the Lord and wept in anguish.'[21] Later verses explain how Hannah was so caught up in expressing herself to God she could barely speak. In fact, her posture and manner were so odd the temple priest assumed she was drunk! But, and here's the beautiful part of the story, God heard Hannah and granted her request for a child. She went on to have several children.

I'm just about done on the subject of prayer, but I think I would be remiss not to touch on one other form of prayer, and that's praise. Praise is an expression of gratitude to and adoration of God, and it is an essential type of prayer for any Christian. The Bible provides us with varied examples of how people have praised God through the ages. King David, one of the most famous Jewish monarchs and the primary author of the psalms, exhorted the people of God to worship Him with music and

---

[21] 1 Samuel 1:10 (NKJV)

dance: 'praise His name with the dance; let them sing praises to Him with the timbrel and harp.'[22]

I want to be clear, I wasn't constantly bursting into song like the character Maria from *The Sound of Music*. There were times when I didn't feel like singing or praising, when the despair weighed me down. But here's the counterintuitive thing about praise: it's most effective in lifting your spirit when you're feeling at your lowest ebb and you feel least like doing it. There's something about reflecting on the power, majesty, and significance of God in praise that helps you to see how small your problems are in comparison. In other words, problems take on their proper dimensions in your eyes.

I fear that I'm doing a poor job of explaining the power of praise. Perhaps that's because it's still something of a mystery to me too. But I can say it's had a transformative effect on me. I think it could do the same for you too.

---

[22] Psalm 149:3 (NKJV)

"The function of prayer is not to influence God,
but rather to change the nature of the one who prays."

— <u>Søren Kierkegaard</u>

CHAPTER 7

Taking a Stand: Capturing and Defending the Battlefield of Your Mind

We started 2011 with the strong conviction that we would suffer no further losses. We had received several prophecies with regard to having children, and we believed them. We were desperate to experience the manifestation of God's promises regarding children. To paraphrase a once popular song, we were sick and tired of being sick and tired!

In November of the previous year, after my husband and I experienced our eleventh miscarriage, the consultants decided to review my treatment, and an appointment was booked for early in the new year. They weren't able to determine the cause of the latest miscarriage, but it was clear that I had not responded sufficiently well to treatment. I was told about a drug that was still on clinical trial for treating recurring miscarriages. The consultant advised that I could use the drug on trial while cautioning me against excessive optimism, as success was not guaranteed.

I was no longer moved by the dire assessments or conclusions of the doctors. Don't get me wrong, I was grateful for their efforts. It's just that as our understanding of the prophetic grew, Seun and I recognised that we needed to spend more time praying for revelation and the strength to persevere and hold on to the promises of God in order to secure victory. I came to a point where, having fully cooperated with the doctors and done all I could when it came to medical assistance, I was content to leave everything in God's hands. My faith was stronger than it had been at the start of the journey. One day during this period, a particular Bible verse came to mind: 'I am leaving you with a gift – peace of mind and heart. And the peace I give is a gift the world cannot give. So don't be troubled or afraid.'[23] I remember being flooded with peace.

My heart was no longer troubled. I believed that God was going to do the miraculous through me just as He had done in the lives of people in the Bible and continues to do in people's lives today. I remembered the story of Sarah in the Bible who was old and past childbearing age but whom God still blessed with a child in her old age. It was a paradox: at the time when things seemed to be darkest, my excitement and faith were at their highest.

This was a long way away from where I started. Something had happened to me as I struggled through this challenge. I had matured spiritually. It had happened so slowly that I hadn't noticed it. My bubbling excitement didn't make me complacent. I knew I was going to have to take certain steps if I wanted anything more tangible. As I stated earlier, my husband and I believed we were

---

[23] John 14:27 (NLT)

engaged in spiritual warfare, and this was where we focused most of our energies.

There was a Bible verse my husband shared with me that reinforced this fighting instinct. The verse captures Isaac's words to his son Esau after it emerged that Jacob (Esau's brother) had cheated him out of the patrimonial blessing he was entitled to as the older sibling: 'And it shall come to pass, when you become restless, that you shall break his yoke from your neck.'[24]

This scripture implies that a breakthrough often requires us to be thoroughly fed up with a recurring challenge and allow our frustration to drive us towards seeking solutions. This wasn't the time to complain or throw my hands up in despair but rather to wrestle with the problem. I no longer wanted to experience losses; I wanted to experience the manifestation of God's promises with regard to children instead.

This faith-based positive outlook triggered certain new behaviours; or rather, it transformed certain negative behaviour patterns. For example, I became a lot more protective of my thought process. I noticed that when I turned on the news, I was often bombarded by a never-ending tide of bad or sad news. Stories of teenagers being stabbed to death, floods destroying homes, growing unemployment, and corporate collapse seemed to abound. Thirty minutes of this sort of sad and bad news was enough to leave me feeling down; a whole day of listening (even if it was simply playing in the background) would leave me completely drained.

---

[24] Genesis 27:41 (NKJV)

Every day, whether we realise it or not, we are bombarded with images and messages conveying both good and bad things. Unfortunately, it's mostly the latter. A deterioration in my well-being seemed a high a price to pay for keeping informed, so I learned to ration my viewing. Obviously, it's important to be aware of what's going on in the world, and listening to the news or reading the newspaper are effective ways of doing that. All I am saying is that I found it very useful for my emotional well-being to manage my intake.

It wasn't just the news, either. I had to cut out some TV programmes altogether. For several years, my husband had expressed consternation at my addiction to a popular British soap opera. Given the unrelenting misery of many of its storylines, he couldn't understand why I liked it so much. He would point out that even when a character in the soap started off happy and content, the plot inevitably darkened and concluded sadly. For my part, I would defend the soap's depiction of life in the UK. I'd argue that dedicating a few hours of my time every week to watching it was merely a way of keeping abreast of real life in our society, even if doing so made me a little sad or depressed at times.

However, once I made the decision to protect my mind, I could no longer justify watching the program. I had to admit that choosing to watch it and making myself sad in the process was not the best use of my time. My decision was validated by the choice of storylines the producers of the soap decided to explore around that time. They'd obviously decided that rather than the run-of-the-mill tragedy they'd been serving up, what was called for was *poignant* tragedy. And the best way to achieve this was to throw a few babies and pregnant women into the mix.

Having made that decision, the programme executed it with gusto; there was infant mortality, miscarriages, and other types of heart-wrenching pregnancy-related mishaps.

The soap's imminent Christmas special was the topic of discussion on one of the popular online pregnancy and parenting forums that I frequently visited. Apparently, the Christmas episode would feature a miscarriage and the kidnapping of a baby. Many of the forum members, especially those who were pregnant or had recently suffered miscarriages, were outraged. Some even argued that the station should not be allowed to air the episode. I didn't join the debate, as I didn't think I had anything novel or insightful to add, but I remember feeling so glad that I had stopped watching the soap.

Experiences such as this showed me the importance of filtering the things I allowed in and strengthened my decision to feed my mind more nourishing food. It's impossible to completely filter out sad news – unexpected events will occur – but while I was facing my own challenges with infertility, I didn't have much room for additional, manufactured sadness.

I wanted to win this battle, and staying mentally strong was an important part of that. In addition to filtering the information that I allowed into my mind, I also had to learn to control the things I allowed my mind to linger on. I had noticed that during my previous pregnancies, thoughts of past negative pregnancy experiences were never far away. If I experienced any bleeding for example, no matter how light the bleeding was, my mind would immediately begin to play out past scenarios in which I had bled and miscarried. It was the most awful feeling of déjà vu, and it had the effect of driving out faith.

I knew I had to learn to master my thoughts. So whenever these negative thoughts came up, I would counter them by verbally declaring the good outcome I was praying for. I would replace the old scenes drawn from memories of past negative experiences with positive ones based on the promises of God. I would do this no matter where I was. By this point, I knew the danger in giving in to fear or negative thoughts driven by bad memories. I was ready to be quite radical about it, and while my tactic of declaring God's promises about fertility out loud might be considered unconventional by some, it worked for me.

I trained my mind to select and focus on positive thoughts over negative ones. My mind was a battlefield, and the thoughts, good and bad, were the soldiers engaged in battle.

If you're at a similar point in your life, my advice would be that you give the devil no opportunity to plant doubt and fear in your mind. Instead, fill your mind with the word of God and His promises to you, as recorded in the Bible. Winning this battle requires constant vigilance. In his second letter to the Corinthians, St. Paul explains how to protect our minds and thoughts. He points out that 'we are destroying speculations and every lofty thing raised up against the knowledge of God, and we are taking every thought captive to the obedience of Christ.'[25] In other words, we need to counter negative speculation and arguments that seek to plant themselves in our minds with words of scripture. No negative thought is too small to address. With constant vigilance, you can win the battle for your mind.

---

[25] 2 Corinthians 10:5 (NASB)

Another important way to protect your mind is by being careful who you discuss your hopes and dreams with. Some people really enjoy pity parties or have picked up the habit of dwelling on negative stories. In my experience, these are the people who always have a tale about a couple who had a painful struggle with infertility before eventually giving up on their dream of having their own biological children. These sorts of stories drain hope. I learned to avoid entering into extended conversation with such people. Sometimes this meant the somewhat drastic step of not taking phone calls from them.

This approach extends beyond coping with infertility. I remember a time, about nine years ago, when I was seeking to change jobs. At the time, I was working at a very small law firm in east London and earning the minimum wage. I wanted a job with a top London firm. When I told one of my friends about this hope of mine, she laughed at me and informed me that it would be extremely difficult for someone of my ethnicity to get a job in the city. She advised me to give up on being a city lawyer and to train in another profession. I didn't argue with her, but I did stop discussing my dreams with her and kept my distance for a while.

Three to six months after that conversation, I got my first job at a top law firm. I've had a few more since. I am still very close to this friend of mind, but at that point in my life, I did not need to keep hearing her negative comments.

"Anything under God's control is never out of control."

— <u>Charles R. Swindoll</u>

CHAPTER 8

Winning the Battle

In April, I became pregnant again. I had mixed feelings. There was certainly excitement, as I was convinced that this pregnancy was the answer to our prayers. But there was also a bit of wariness about the potential emotional turbulence that lay ahead. 'Will this pregnancy be free of trouble?' I wondered to myself.

This wasn't because I didn't have faith. On the contrary, I was full of faith. Having said that, I knew my adversary, and as the Bible says, we should not be ignorant of the devil's devices. Faith doesn't preclude a realistic assessment of a situation. I know Christians who (figuratively) beat themselves up for lacking faith because they are honest about their situation. I would like to encourage anyone who's ever done that by sharing my understanding of faith and what it isn't. Faith is not deluding oneself about the size of a challenge, it's about being able to properly access it in the light of God's power and love.

My desire was to experience a turbulence-free pregnancy. After my pregnancy had been confirmed, I contacted the Recurrent Miscarriage Clinic and ultrasound scans were scheduled. At the first ultrasound scan, we heard the baby's heartbeat. I was so excited. But even in the midst of my excitement, doubt whispered warnings in my ear: 'Don't connect too much with this baby; remember what happened in the past.'

As I mentioned earlier, I'd learned some of the ways the devil operates. Isolation and secrecy are two of his keys tools. So I wasted no time in sharing the doubts plaguing my mind with my husband and mentors. They reminded me of how far I had come and helped me see that my faith would win out over fear.

My husband and I didn't just seek the encouragement of other believers – we sought their support in prayer, too. Our church pastors had committed to praying with us throughout this pregnancy. It was quite astonishing but also very touching to learn that almost everyone was praying along with us, even church members who were not close friends. This reminded me of the stories of believers in the early church and their practice of sharing and praying together. When St. Peter was arrested, the Bible notes that the church earnestly prayed for him until he was freed from prison. The book of Acts states, 'So Peter was kept in jail but the people of the church were praying earnestly for him.'[26]

I have come to the realisation that spiritual battles, like physical ones, are more easily won when you're part of an army rather than a lone hero warrior. This corporate act of love taught me the importance of praying more consistently for other people, especially those facing challenges on their way to parenthood.

Six weeks into the pregnancy, the bleeding started and got progressively heavier. The painful stomach cramps also started. Even when I began to bleed, at around the same point (six

---

[26] Acts 12:5 (GNT)

weeks into the pregnancy) that I'd bled during, and ultimately lost, my previous pregnancies, my husband and I remained focused. We were determined not to be moved by it. I would constantly tell myself things like 'The blood is not my baby, my baby is fine' and 'My baby is firmly attached to my uterine wall.' I also repeated Bible verses such as, 'No one shall suffer miscarriage or be barren in your land; I will fulfill the number of your days'[27] to myself. My primary reason for making these affirmative statements over and over again was to quieten the negative thoughts and their power to induce fear in me. In other words, I needed to keep my eyes on God and His promises, not the problem.

This battle for my mind resulted in some funny episodes. I remember walking home from the train station one evening, not thinking about anything in particular, when out of nowhere a terrible thought popped into my mind: 'The bleeding has not stopped yet, and the pregnancy is still in the early stages. I might lose it.' I immediately verbally decried this thought, oblivious of the gentleman walking beside me. I remember saying in a loud and firm voice, 'No way! My baby is fine. I will *not* miscarry, and this pregnancy will be carried to full term.' The poor man walking next me was so startled he jumped.

I can imagine some people reading this and thinking my behaviour was a bit extreme. Perhaps it was, and I completely accept that not everyone will be comfortable with this approach; but to my mind, this was an effective way of fighting for control of my mind and ultimately my future.

---

[27] Exodus 23:26 (NIV)

Earlier in the year, I had developed the habit of spending between two and three hours praying and meditating on Bible verses in the early hours of every day. That habit stood me in good stead now. Whenever I felt the painful cramps, I would take painkillers, but I would also recall Bible verses and insights from the books I had read. I did this continually because I was determined not to give any room to fear, doubt, or unbelief. I held onto my belief that this pregnancy would be our breakthrough.

I would repeatedly say to myself, 'Kemi, you're not afraid of the blood loss. Your baby is intact and firmly attached to the uterine wall.' I got very specific in my pronouncements. I reported the bleeding and large blood clots to the sonographer during my regular ultrasound scans at the RMC, but she saw no indication of bleeding in the womb, and the foetus was growing fine.

I believed God was setting us up for a miracle, though I felt physically weak from the blood loss and the pain. This pregnancy, the twelfth one, was going to be the game-changer. After the ten-week scan, I was referred from the clinic to the hospital where I planned to have my baby for my antenatal care.

The consultants and specialist nurses who'd been caring for me at the RMC were amazed at the progress of this pregnancy. On one occasion, one of the consultants asked me what I was doing differently this time, as everything seemed to be going so well. I was so full of the wonder of what God was doing that my testimony of faith in Jesus came pouring out. I'm still not quite sure what he made of that!

The twelve-week scan is often referred to as the 'dating' scan, as it's the first scan at which doctors are able to estimate the baby's birthdate. As my dating scan drew closer, I was excited, but I was also exhausted by the constant bleeding and cramps I'd been experiencing all through the pregnancy. I desperately wanted to enjoy being pregnant. I began to pray that the bleeding and cramps would stop. Two days later, they did.

My twelve-week scan was a wonderful and beautiful experience, unmarred by any pain or bleeding. I asked for a picture of my baby. I stared at the picture all through the journey home from the hospital. During my previous pregnancies, I'd never requested a picture because the ultrasound scans always showed the signs of potential miscarriages. This time, my baby was fine. There was no fear in my heart, and I was looking forward to every week of the advancing pregnancy.

All through this time, our mentors and pastors prayed with us for a healthy and a full-term pregnancy. In particular, the senior church pastor prayed and anointed me with oil every fortnight after the church service. My faith affected my demeanour, so much so that my pastor remarked that he'd never seen me smile so much.

Once my baby bump became noticeable, I took to observing it keenly for any changes. Week after week, I would ask my husband whether he thought my bump was showing more. I took countless pictures of my baby bump. I was excited about seeing it grow, knowing that I was getting closer and closer to meeting our son, the 'breakthrough baby.' He was making his way into the world against all odds.

When I wasn't incessantly asking my husband for his views on my bump or taking pictures of it, I was standing in front of the mirror staring at it, wondering in amazement at God's handiwork and the changes my body was making to accommodate it. I was so enchanted by the experience, it's surprising that I got anything else done!

To top it all off, I experienced no morning sickness. The rest of my pregnancy was stress-free. When I was about sixteen weeks into my pregnancy, I shared my happy news with my friends from the online forum I frequented. Over a period of about two years, I had developed a friendship with a group of women from this forum. Like me, they had been struggling to conceive or carry a pregnancy full-term. We had shared our stories of heartbreak and hope as well as joy. We'd gotten excited together, prayed together, and shared Bible verses while encouraging one other.

By happy coincidence, about five of us became pregnant around the same time. It was brilliant to be able to see the scans and baby-bump pictures that others posted. We continued to pray for one another, especially those who were still trying to get pregnant or carry to term.

I did not post pictures online, as my husband and I had decided to share the good news with only a few people – our pastors, our mentors, and a small group of friends and family. We weren't motivated by fear in this regard but by a desire not to stress out a number of loved ones.

Being pregnant didn't just change the way my body looked, it also changed the foods I liked and my appetite in general. I didn't feel like eating much, and when I did feel like eating, I was no longer tempted by my favourite foods: rice with beef or chicken curry. Instead, I craved Marks and Spencer's egg and watercress sandwiches – only Marks and Spencer's would do. Also, I developed a taste for the cheese and ham paninis sold in the hospital canteen. Whenever I visited the hospital for my antenatal care, I would buy a ham and cheese panini and a mug of hot chocolate. It was pure bliss; cheese and ham had never tasted so good. I also developed a strange penchant for crunching ice cubes even in chilly weather. They tasted so good to me.

I don't know if these cravings were the result of hormonal changes or whether the old wives' tale of pregnancy cravings gave me the excuse to indulge hitherto subconscious food desires, but I enjoyed every minute of it.

Meanwhile, my husband excitedly drew up lists of potential baby names. He told me he wanted a meaningful Greek name for our child and asked one of his Greek colleagues to suggest a few possibilities. We attended antenatal classes together. This turned out to be a big help after our baby was born, as Seun was perfectly able to care for our son. He even pointed out things I missed.

I received brilliant care from the hospital throughout my pregnancy. I was placed on a high-risk care programme due to my previous recurrent miscarriages and the blood-thinning medication I was on. Several of the medical staff expressed surprise that we had persevered for so long. They asked how I found the strength to keep trying through eleven pregnancy losses. I wish I'd taken the opportunity to tell them about the blessings of God and His faithfulness. I wish I'd explained how God sustained me, but all I said at the time was that we'd been on a long journey and were happy to finally get to this point. This was true, but it did not do justice to our story or God's role in it.

One of my favourite books during my twelfth pregnancy was one titled *Supernatural Childbirth*. I read this book several times. I found that it not only encouraged me to persevere but also gave me lovely little insights into pregnancy and childbirth.

The author, Jackie Mize, provided a lot of advice to expectant mothers on some of the things to consider praying about during the various stages of pregnancy.

When the time came to deliver my baby, I got off to a bit of a bumpy start. Although I was experiencing strong contractions, my cervix wasn't dilating fast enough. Six hours in, I was only about three centimetres dilated. You might think that with all I had learned about prayer and spiritual warfare, I'd have launched into prayer straightaway, but you'd be wrong.

At this point, I turned to my husband and tearfully explained that I didn't think I'd be able to go through the ordeal of a natural birth. It was taking too long, and I was getting tired. Seun had been an absolute superstar throughout the process. When he wasn't telling me how well I was doing, he was praying quietly. When he saw I was flagging, he reminded me of the journey of faith I'd been on throughout this pregnancy and all that we had been through together. He also reminded me about a passage from *Supernatural Childbirth* that had covered the importance of praying for a drama-free labour (I'm paraphrasing; the author didn't put it quite like that).

At that point, the gynaecologist consultant who had come to check on me informed us that if I did not progress into labour by the end of that day, the medical team would perform a caesarean section (C-section). I was keen to avoid a C-section if I could. There are many good reasons that a doctor might propose or a woman might opt to have a C-section, but it is not without its shortcomings. My primary reason for wanting to avoid one is the potentially slow post-operative recovery process. Besides, while C-sections aren't uncommon (about one in four births in the UK is via Caesarean[28]), they are still major surgical procedure, and as such carry a risk of complications, albeit a small risk in countries such as the UK.

Anyway, on hearing the doctor's words, I decided that I couldn't wait any longer, and I called out to God in prayer. I asked Him to make my cervix dilate enough for me to deliver my baby without complications or any further delays. And my prayer was answered almost immediately, because to the surprise of the midwife, less than two hours later my cervix was fully dilated.

When the time came to push, every bit of my lower body felt the pressure to deliver my baby. I had this surge of energy and a sense of excitement about meeting our long-awaited miracle baby. I don't remember feeling any pain by this point (then again, I was in a bit of a daze), but I do remember the words of the medical team: *push, good work, hold on, don't stop*, and then the magical one, *congratulations*. Was a more beautiful word ever uttered? He was finally here!

Once my son was born, the pain of the labour faded into insignificance compared to the other feelings that were welling up within me. My husband and I were filled with joy to overflowing and couldn't take our eyes off him. And who could blame us? He was obviously the cutest baby in the history of the world.

I do not have the words to describe how it felt to hold our precious bundle against my skin. Handing him over so that my husband could fix our son's first nappy and ease him into his oversized BabyGro was a wrench. We took pictures, hugged,

---

[28] 'Caesarean Birth: NCT Position Statement,' the NCT, http://www.nct.org.uk/sites/default/files/related_documents/NCT%20position%20statement%20CaesareanBirth_1.pdf.

kissed, and held our bundle of joy, who looked undeniably like his dad. Meanwhile, my mother, who had been present during the birth, was literally rolling about on the floor singing praises to God. It was both a hilarious and a moving sight. I knew that if I had been able to move, I'd have been doing the same thing; as it was, I was singing praises from the bottom of my heart.

"Patience can be bitter but her fruit is always sweet."

— <u>Habeeb Akande</u>

CHAPTER 9

My Exceedingly Great Reward

The situations we are confronted with in life have an amazing ability to mould our understanding of who we are and who we think God is. I have come out of my struggle with infertility with a better understanding of both. This knowledge has made me stronger and more emotionally stable. It has also given me a whole new perspective on facing challenges.

I started out on the journey of faith I have described in this book seeking a child, but along the way I found so much more. In this I can see parallels between my experience and that of Abraham, the spiritual father of the Christian faith. The book of Genesis records a conversation between Abram (later Abraham) and God, in which God assures him, 'I am your shield, your exceedingly great reward.'[29]

God's assurance is met with consternation from Abraham who, unable to understand how he could be a blessed man without a biological heir, responded: 'Sovereign Lord, what can you give me since I remain childless and the one who will inherit

---

[29] Genesis 15:1 (NKJV)

my estate is Eliezer of Damascus? ... You have given me no children; so a servant in my household will be my heir.' Later in the conversation, God promises Abraham not just a biological child but a multitude of descendants.

Abraham believed God and his relationship with God evolved in light of this promise. While awaiting the promised child, Abraham experienced both ups and downs, but all the way through he believed God. And it was because of Abraham's determined wait in the face of these ups and downs that he was described as a righteous man.

His long wait was not in vain. Abraham eventually had a son called Isaac, through whom the nation of Israel was ultimately birthed. But even more than the fulfilment of the promise, Abraham got to know God.

On my way to having children, my relationship with God has evolved in ways that would have been unlikely if I hadn't been facing such a difficult challenge. Like father Abraham, I've come to know God, and by extension I've developed a better understanding of who I am. I've learned to worry less and trust Him more.

I have also learned about the power of pain to clarify and to act as a propellant. The key is to push through rather than let it stop you. My pain has helped me to see and embark on one of my life's purposes: supporting couples going through infertility. I didn't know it at the time, but there was purpose in the pain.

Purpose, even in painful or distressing experiences, is one of the outcomes the Bible promises to those who trust in God's redemptive ability: 'We know that God causes everything to work together for the good of those who love God and are called according to his purpose for them.'[30]

In my case, some of the ways that my experiences have worked together for the good include inner strength, an ability to faithfully persevere, and an expectation of good things from God. It is in the light of this expectation that I'm able to enjoy or endure the different seasons of life. The Bible explains that there is a time for everything:

> For everything there is a season, a time for every activity under heaven. A time to plant and a time to harvest. Yet God has made everything beautiful for its own time. He has planted eternity in the human heart, but even so, people cannot see the whole scope of God's work from beginning to end; Ecclesiastes 3:1–2, 11 (NLT).

Experiences are no longer the barometer for my relationship with God. In the past, I assessed God's love for me in light of the things I faced. I was assured of God's love when things were going well and became angry, bewildered, or insecure when they weren't. Today my perspective on life is based on an expectation of God's faithfulness, and it's an expectation borne of experience. This knowledge sustained me and has transformed how I view the challenges I face. The Bible describes this in a beautifully eloquent language:

---

[30] Romans 8:28 (NLT)

We can rejoice, too, when we run into problems and trials, for we know that they help us develop endurance. And endurance develops strength of character, and character strengthens our confident hope of salvation. And this hope will not lead to disappointment. For we know how dearly God loves us, because he has given us the Holy Spirit to fill our hearts with his love; Romans 5:3–6 (NLT).

My husband and I have achieved victory over our seemingly impossible challenge. Our almost six year-long season of waiting came to an end. Today, when we look at our child who is now a toddler and is full of energy and curiosity, we can't help but wonder at this gift. He is an endless source of pleasant surprises. He was well worth the wait.

I started this journey seeking a child, but along the way I found mentors, friends, wisdom, and most importantly, God. My son is a brilliant gift – one that just keeps on giving – but God is my exceedingly great reward.

"Experience is not what happens to you. It is what you do with what happens to you. Don't waste your pain; use it to help others."
— Rick Warren, _The Purpose Driven Life: What on Earth Am I Here for?_

Appendix

In this book, I've shared my battle with infertility. The experience provided me with an opportunity to meet some extraordinary women and hear their stories. We drew strength from one another, and they have kindly agreed to share their stories so that readers of this book can draw strength too.

Infertility is such an uncomplicated word. It's the opposite of fertility – what could be simpler? But it describes a complicated, multifaceted issue. For some infertile couples, the problem is an inability to conceive; for others, the struggle is carrying a baby to full-term; and for some, no medical cause is ever diagnosed. So while the pain and heartache are the same, the causes and types of infertility vary. The ways those of us who have faced this challenge have chosen to deal with it also vary.

I wanted to give readers of this book some insight into the different issues and approaches of others who have grappled with infertility. These are their stories.

The Adoption Story

My husband and I have two sons. We got married in August 1997 without any rigid plans for parenthood, but we knew we wanted children as soon as possible. We waited eleven years for our first miracle baby. He came into our lives in 2008 through adoption. Our second miracle baby arrived in 2011, via the more conventional, biological route!

During the eleven-year wait between our wedding and carrying our first son in our arms, we tried so many different medical treatments. Our hopes were raised and disappointed so many times. Emotionally, the treatments were very draining for both my husband and I. The entire experience was a roller-coaster. We'd be full of hope at the start of each medical treatment – believing, each time, that this would be the one that would work. Then there were times when we felt deeply discouraged, when yet another treatment did not work. There was the pain of seeing friends who had married after us having children. And then there was acceptance. We came to the conclusion that if children didn't come, it wasn't the end of the world. We had each other, and that was all that mattered.

The challenge made our marriage stronger. We felt God was always with us in this journey, and His promises would be fulfilled in our lives. What sustained us was knowing that we had each other, and everything was in God's hands. So why worry? We occupied ourselves with volunteering in our local church and doing other things we enjoyed in spite of our situation. This experience drew us closer to God and helped us accept God as the all-knowing one.

The decision to adopt our son was one that filled us with joy. For us, the desire to show love to a child was stronger than the insistence that it must be our own biological child. Apart from the strong feeling to give our love to a child, the trigger was the inner peace that it was what God wanted us to do, and we did not feel like we had given up. He is a beautiful child, and we continue to feel blessed to have him in our lives. He made our experience of parenthood both enjoyable and profound.

We were fully immersed in this joyful experience when I became pregnant naturally. Yet more great news – another addition to our family! A beautiful toddler and a baby on the way; what more could we ask for? The miracle of this conception in the face of several attempts over the years was evidence of God's faithfulness. My pregnancy was perfect, no illness, and delivery was a wonderful experience – only thirty minutes in labour. I honestly could not ask for more.

My advice to those still waiting and hoping to have children would be this: Don't put your life on hold while you are waiting. Hold on to God's words and be comforted. Choose not to be miserable. Enjoy spending time with the children of others. If God leads you to adopt a child, do it! Adoption has been such an amazing and fulfilling experience for us.

My journey through infertility into motherhood with two lovely boys has made me realise that truly, there is nothing that God cannot do. I would like to leave you with some words from the book of Habakkuk: 'For the vision is yet for an appointed time, but at the end it shall speak and not lie: Though it tarries, wait for it, because it will surely come, it will not tarry.[31]'

---

[31] Habakkuk 2:3 (NKJV)

Overcoming Infertility Caused by
Polycystic Ovarian Syndrome (PCOS)

We got married July 2009. We planned on starting a family immediately, but in the end it took two years and ten months. Our experience during those two years was difficult, most especially because we'd planned on starting a family immediately. After a year of trying without success, I was referred to a gynaecologist. All sorts of tests were carried out. It took a whole year to get a diagnosis.

Apparently, I was suffering from Polycystic Ovarian Syndrome. PCOS is a condition that affects a woman's menstrual cycle and her ability to have children. My periods had always been irregular and short; in other words, my ovulation was irregular. I was prescribed various drugs to help my body to ovulate

It was while I was coming to grips with the implications of this diagnosis that I was made redundant at work. Losing my job was a big blow to my faith. Being at home while seeking new employment was tedious and draining. I was often bored and had a lot of time to dwell on my challenge. I felt everything was wrong with me, and I was in a constant state of sadness. I became extremely emotional, and every morning during my personal devotion time I would cry even while asking God for strength. I was so discouraged by my circumstances.

Through it all, my husband was a quiet tower of strength. He never showed any negative emotions, nor was he downcast when we talked about it. He was constantly encouraging. At other times, he would call my mum and ask her to encourage me when he could see I was feeling down.

As a believer, I trusted that God would work things out and I would eventually have a child or even children, but I couldn't help but wonder how long the wait was going to be. It was in the midst of this challenge that I received a prophecy, during a special prayer session in church, that God was going to bless my husband and I with children very soon. I held on to those words, and as an act of faith I started shopping for baby clothes. Gradually, I began to develop a closer relationship with God. I spent more time in prayer and Bible study, and I continued to believe God's promises about the gift of children.

Despite this, the medication didn't seem to be working. My husband and I were informed that if my body did not respond to the treatment, I would have to be referred to a fertility clinic. After a while, it seemed that the fertility clinic, more tests, and more treatments would be the inevitable next steps. And then one day, at my new place of employment, I took ill and had to be rushed to the nearest hospital. In the course of some routine tests, the doctors found out I was six weeks pregnant! I was in so much shock and amazement at the answer to my prayers. After all, just a few months ago I had been informed by the doctors that I was not responding to the ovulation drugs and they were looking to refer me to the fertility clinic for assisted conception.

My pregnancy and delivery were both complication-free. I had no morning sickness, no big swollen feet, no headaches. My labour lasted just twenty minutes, and I didn't need any pain relief. I could see that God was completely in charge. I received my heart's desire.

I know that advising those going through infertility not to worry is trite and often unhelpful, so I won't do it here. But I will say, find useful outlets for your energies. For me, it was preparing for my baby. This was more than a way to keep me occupied, it was also an act of faith. So my advice is prepare for your baby: buy baby clothes and feeding bottles, and when you are feeling down, let them help you focus your prayers. For example, pray that you will get to put them all to use with your baby. Secondly, I'd advise that you find ways to occupy your mind. I chose to focus on the word of God. I stuck Bible verses all over my bedroom. My favourites were from the book of Psalms: Psalm 128:3, Psalm 127:3–5, and Psalm 113:9. I hope they will encourage you too.

Infertility Caused by Blocked Tubes and Adhesions to the Womb

I got married to the love of my life on November 11, 2008. I was 100 percent sure that I would get pregnant within a month. But month after month, nothing happened. We waited three years before the birth of our beautiful twin girls in November 2011. Our girls were born a couple of weeks shy of our third wedding anniversary. They were the best anniversary present.

I'm not sure where to start in telling this story, but I think it's important to say I had so much support from my husband and immediate family, but I found the reaction of wider society awful. Nigerian society can be so unsympathetic when it comes to infertility. The careless comments and innuendos from some colleagues and distant acquaintances cut deep.

By the end of our first year of marriage, I'd had a laparoscopy and a hysteroscopy, and then I found out my right tube was partially blocked. Adhesions from an earlier myomectomy further compounded the problem. The adhesions were cleared, and I was placed on Clomid, a fertility drug, but it didn't work. We didn't give up, though. After trying Clomid one more time, we decided to consider other forms of medical intervention.

Infertility took over my life. I breathed, ate, slept, and talked about it all the time. It even affected my work, as I found myself on the Internet most of the time, reading every and any article I could find on infertility. I became so well informed about my condition that my doctor used to joke that I was knowledgeable enough to come work for him.

Infertility affected me in other ways, too. For example, I retreated into my shell socially. Luckily, my husband was my solid rock, and we were a tag-team all the way. I took so many things out on him, but he always understood. He always let me cry, vent, or lament.

He wasn't perfect though. He also frustrated me with his stubbornness sometimes. He wasn't always quick to 'cooperate' during my fertile moments, and he'd complain about the lack of spontaneity in our sex life. So we had arguments almost every time I ovulated.

Infertility was the hardest journey I ever took. It was very frustrating. I swung between rock solid faith that something surely had to happen someday to crying and asking God why He had abandoned me and was punishing me in this way. Sometimes I would pray and fast fervently; at other times, I would rebel and refuse to utter a word of prayer for days. Yet through it all, God was my sustenance. I got the most comfort from leaning on Him and His word. My husband and mother were also fantastic. I had to learn blind trust. By this I mean that I learned to believe even when I couldn't see.

And then I became pregnant. I was elated, but two days after my positive pregnancy test, I started spotting. I was terrified until a blood test confirmed I was still pregnant. I spotted almost all through my first trimester. At nine weeks, I even had blood clots. At that point, I was convinced it was all over. The spotting stopped only after I had a cervical stitch put in at thirteen weeks.

My experience of pregnancy wasn't all about spotting scares; there were upsides, too. For example, after a very minor bout of morning sickness in the first couple of weeks, I was bursting with good health and vibrancy. I had so much energy, I was able to take a trip to the United States in the twenty-sixth week of my pregnancy. In my third trimester, I had to slow down a bit, as I got so huge and was a bit anaemic. At exactly thirty-seven weeks, my beautiful girls were born via C-section. All I can say is that this faithful, promise-keeping God is so amazing!

I look back on my journey through infertility and there are lessons that I think others might benefit from too. Firstly, draw on your spouse's strength and allow him to do the same for you. You're at your strongest when you operate as a team. Seal your love and mutual support by praying together. It's you two against the world.

Secondly, be informed. Know what's going on with your body. This knowledge helps drive out fear, which thrives where there is ignorance, and it helps you become firm friends with your doctor. Don't live in blind ignorance.

Thirdly and finally, try not to worry. Instead, trust God. Remember the words of St. Paul to the church in Phillipi: 'Do not be anxious about anything, but in every situation, by prayer and petition, with thanksgiving, present your requests to God. And the peace of God, which transcends all understanding, will guard your hearts and your minds in Christ Jesus.'[32]

Battling Recurring Late-Stage Miscarriages

We got married in February 1999, and we had planned to start a family a year after we got married. It took us eight years and seven months before we had our first child, and a further three years after that before we eventually had our second son.

Back in 1999, we had no idea that it would take us so long or that becoming parents would be such an emotionally exhausting experience. In fact, I became pregnant for the first time just six weeks into our marriage. I travelled to Sierra Leone for my grandmother's funeral when I was six months pregnant, and while there I felt enough pain to warrant a trip to the hospital. It was there that I was informed that my baby had been dead for at least twenty-four hours prior to my admission. We were shattered, confused, and words could not describe the sudden blow we felt.

I was still emotionally raw from the first miscarriage when in 2000, I became pregnant again – this time with twins. Tragedy struck at the twenty-ninth week into the pregnancy, a second ultrasound revealed that one of the twins, seen in an earlier scan was 'missing'. Then I was diagnosed with malaria and whilst on treatment for malaria, I went into labour and had a stillbirth. I'd lost the second child.

---

[32] Philippians 4:6–7 (NIV)

I was so hurt and despairing, I didn't want to be comforted, especially by those closest to me. Having to explain the situation to neighbours and work colleagues who had seen me pregnant and asked to see the baby was an additional pain to bear. My husband would protect me by asking close relatives to refrain from being mournful around me.

In 2002, I became pregnant for the third time. This time it was preeclampsia that struck. Preeclampsia is a condition that, if left untreated, can result in full-blown eclampsia and brain seizures in pregnant women. High blood pressure and high urine protein levels are both indicators of preeclampsia. The causes of the condition vary, but the only 'cures' are induced labour or a C-section. I had to deliver my baby early while he was still very premature. Unfortunately, he died two days later.

By the time I became pregnant for the fourth time, in 2004, I had moved to the United Kingdom from Pakistan. In my twenty-sixth week, during an antenatal visit, it was discovered that my blood pressure was quite high, and I had to be admitted into the hospital immediately. The doctors were surprised I had not experienced any of the symptoms I should have. I'd experienced no swelling of the feet or face, no dizziness or severe headaches.

I was admitted and diagnosed with placenta praevia. This is the term given to a placenta that's lying low in the uterus and probably covering part or the whole of the cervix (the entrance to the womb). An emergency Caesarean section was performed, and once again my baby was stillborn. The hospital wanted to perform a hysterectomy, which is a surgical removal of the womb. Although I was doing poorly, I refused the procedure, and another consultant intervened and argued against the procedure being carried out.

At this point, the longest I had carried a pregnancy was thirty-two weeks and the earliest point at which I have lost a pregnancy was twenty-five weeks (I had lost four boys and a girl).

Every loss was traumatic, and I became very depressed. I don't think I've ever cried as much. The fact that my husband was in Nigeria because he hadn't received his visa to join me in the UK made things worse. It was hard dealing with the careless comments of colleagues and even some friends. It was difficult to bear the stigma of being the couple who lost their babies all by myself. There were so many times that I didn't feel like praying. I even put my career on hold.

Strangely, the heartbreak drew my husband and I closer as a couple. Somehow, we continued to look forward to becoming devoted parents, and we prayed for other people who wanted to have children too. We continued to trust God had a purpose in all of this. We were very lucky to have the support of our parents, mentors, a few faithful friends and 'fruit of the womb' support group. I don't know what we'd have done without them.

The challenge tested my faith in God. It pushed me. It also drew me closer to my church family. My husband and I had been a Sunday school teachers to young children since our teen years, a role we have enjoyed till date. We were assured someday that our own kids would be in the congregation of God's people. During this period, I found a particular Bible verse very helpful: 'He grants the barren woman a home, like a joyful mother of children. Praise the Lord!'[33] A pool of trusted friends constantly prayed with us and for us.

When I finally got pregnant in 2007, my pregnancy was so smooth, but I was also very careful. My advice to others, for what it's worth, is to continue to hold on to God's word and lean on those people who want to support you – and that includes your spouse. Don't go through it alone. Also, seek medical opinions so you are knowledgeable about what you are up against. My favourite scriptures were Exodus 23:25 and 26, Psalms118:17 and Isaiah 49:25b. I hope you find them comforting and faith-building too.

---

[33] Psalm 113:9 (NIV)

If you enjoyed reading this book, please send
your comments and testimonies.
Thank you.

**For Speaking Engagements, Questions and Enquiries
Contact Me Directly**

Email: justaseaon@beulahcreations.com
Telephone: +44 (0) 79034 37615 (UK)